This Is the Day
Finding Your Calling for Christ

Devotional

JAIMEE WOLFARD

ISBN 979-8-88616-598-2 (paperback)
ISBN 979-8-88616-599-9 (digital)

Christian Faith Publishing
832 Park Avenue
Meadville, PA 16335
www.christianfaithpublishing.com

Printed in the United States of America

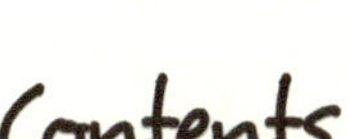

Contents

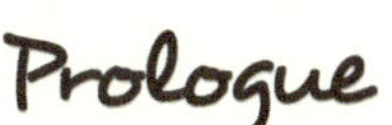

Prologue

Today, I listened. Today, I made a choice. Today is a new beginning.

Have you ever had a dream? Not just a dream while in REM sleep but a dream for your future? Let's go one step deeper.

Have you ever had a dream of God's future for you? A passion so evident that when spoken of you feel a tightening inside your chest, you well up with tears, and you find it so overwhelming you have to stop talking about it because you feel it is too much for you? Have you ever come to the conclusion that you aren't good enough to accomplish your dream? Have you ever said "This is a great idea. I will help someone do this if it is brought up because there is no way I could lead it. There is no way I have time"? Well, you are not alone. My dreams began over fifteen years ago.

Let me start by introducing myself. I am simply a wife, a mother, a teacher, a worship team member, and a caregiver. I know there are so many more hats that I wear, but this gives you the main idea of what I do on a daily basis. There are so many things that I attend to in order to keep things running smoothly in every avenue of my life.

Unfortunately, many times, something suffers. See, I am not perfect, nor am I a superwoman. I get weary, disappointed, complacent, sad as well as all those opposites: energetic, joyful, proud, and longing for the next step. This is where I am at in my life. I had become so weary in doing well, sad with where I was in my complacency that I decided to make a change. I was tired of the mundane. I began to long for the next step, for something more. That desire is what led me to begin this journey.

Many years ago, God came to me in a dream, and I saw a moment of my life that had shadows of people. The faces were missing from bodies, but there were crowds of people. I could see myself on a stage with a microphone. I didn't know what it meant, but I just prayed about it. A few years later, I had the exact same dream again.

I quickly began praying and asking God to show me what it meant and who the people were on the stage with me. He wasn't answering, so I stopped praying about it. I felt it was too big of a dream for me to conquer on my own, and I felt as if God wasn't responding. I mean, really, there wasn't much to go on; no audible voice, no prophet sent with a message at those times—so I "shelved it." That's a term I teach my students: to shelve it for later. It means to take those thoughts that are pressing on your mind and imagine that you are placing them on a shelf until you are ready to readdress the issue.

So I did. Many seasons of my life passed, and God allowed me to have this same dream again. Nothing new; no changes. "Why? If I don't know the next step, how am I supposed to take it?" That was all I continued to ask.

Isn't that what we all want? We want the steps planned out and clearly given to us so we can easily just do it. Just do it—that was the issue. I didn't feel like I could do anything, and I felt completely unprepared for what I thought I was supposed to do. How was I supposed to know what to do with the passion, the tightening of my chest and the tearful moments I had when I would talk about it with someone? God wasn't playing audibles, and I felt confused.

In this book, I am going to share what God has birthed in me and the battle of the flesh that we all have. I hope to give you revelation to see what God's steps are for your dream, your calling to come to fruition. You have a greater life in store for you as a chosen child, adopted into the kingdom of God. There is an alignment that we all need to have before God will show us our next step. Waiting for it doesn't make it happen, but I will share with you what God revealed to me.

I pray that as you read this devotional you will allow God to reveal His purpose and expectations of you and that you can then say "This is the day I listened, chose, and began to live out my greater life."

Testimony: The Rest of the Story

Several years back (2005), my husband and I prayed about taking a position as worship pastors at a church out of state. We fully believed that this was the direction for our lives. We were going to have to sell our home prior to the move, but my husband was going ahead of the family to begin ministering as I stayed back to sell our home. We had three little ones who stayed with me: Josiah, who at that time was five years old; Elijah, two years old; and Molly Selah, who was one year old. Life was about to turn a one-eighty on us.

After having Molly, I had some clogged glands in my armpit. They were causing lymph nodes to be inflamed and my armpit to swell. After several months of phone calls and appointments, the doctor decided to surgically remove the axillary tissue.

Less than a week after my surgery, on the Saturday prior to the Monday my husband was moving out of state, I received a phone call from my surgeon's office. We all know that they don't make calls on the weekend unless it is urgent. Our best friends were over, spending some quality time with us prior to Atlee leaving, when I received the call. My friend has worked in the medical field all her adult life, and I asked her what her thoughts were on the Saturday call. She very calmly stated that it must be important. You see, they asked me to not let my husband leave Monday morning because they needed us to come in to speak to the surgeon. My thoughts ran rampant at that moment, but I got a grip and continued through the weekend as if I never had received a call.

On Monday morning, with my husband and father-in-law packed and ready to head to New Mexico from Missouri for this next season of our lives, we went to the surgeon's office to find out what the "urgent" news was. The doctor proceeded to tell us that within my axillary tissue there was a 2.5-inch tumor that was tested and diagnosed to be the most aggressive form of breast cancer at that

time (HER/2neu). We asked what our next step would be, and he proceeded to confirm what we were thinking. There would be chemotherapy and radiation as well as another surgery. After he told us that he would be following a protocol that had the best outcomes, he gave us the devastating news that the life span with this protocol was still only two to five years.

Knowing I was diagnosed with cancer and given a bleak outlook on life, I had a few things I needed to say to my husband. I was not prepared to be a warrior at that moment. I hadn't even thought about *how* I would respond, but I never backed down from worshipping God and talking to Him. The doctor left the room downtrodden and allowed us to have a few minutes alone.

I took a deep breath, paused to gather my thoughts, and told him the three things I felt he needed to know right then. I said, "Well, I told you that while we were apart, I was going to lose some weight and now it sounds like I could. I also told you I was going to get a new hairdo, but this won't be exactly what I was thinking on style." I giggled as he continued to frown, then I said that I was sorry because I was not going to be able to get tanned since I couldn't be out in the sun much during chemotherapy.

He told me to stop and to get serious. I told him I was and that God had ordained our steps. He knew exactly what we had been praying for, and he knew the battle we faced in making the decision to uproot our lives and move. I told him that we were not changing our minds just because the devil threw a wrench in our plans.

You see, I had already read that part of the Bible before. In John 10:10 (ESV), Jesus says, "The thief comes only to steal and kill and destroy. I came that they may have life and have it abundantly." God told us that the devil would be scheming to destroy us and the ministry that God has for us. I was not about to let the devil win.

We shared the news with my father-in-law, then we all prayed in the parking garage. I reaffirmed God's strength in us to my husband, and they left from the doctor's office to move my husband on from Missouri to New Mexico. From there, I began using the first tool I had to become the warrior I was to be in order to beat the news the doctor had given me: the Bible. With God's guide in my hand, I was determined to find the strategies to move forward and find my healing. I was determined to be trained for this war and become a warrior from that day forward.

The battle wasn't easy, but with my armor on, I kept warring. I was determined to be a warrior for God, especially during this season of my life. I was fighting for my life, for my children, for my husband, and for my faith to be built up and strengthened daily. I encouraged others to glorify God daily for my healing. There was to be no pity. I had my mind made up that I didn't want it because I was going to see a victory. I tried to continue my normal routines of life, and that became overwhelming. I refused to let the devil have my worship.

In the beginning of the battle, I lost the use of my left arm due to cording from the surgery. I could only raise my hand at the wrist. Guess what? I raised that hand during worship. I was not going to stop praising my Jesus, my healer. I had to go through strenuous physical therapy, and with every small improvement of my arm, I would lift it a little higher. I would worship and lift my arm as high as I could until I was in full extension again.

The devil did not win, so he tried again. It wasn't long after this, lymphedema formed in my left breast from the radiation I had undergone. Although I was going through physical therapy for this as well, the lymphedema moved up my neck and was choking my vocal cords. I sounded like I had laryngitis with only a whisper.

At first, I felt defeated. The doctors told me that it would be permanent due to the chemotherapy protocol. I cried, feeling like I had nothing left to give Jesus. I thought my identity was being taken from me. As soon as I heard myself say those words, I put myself in check. My identity is in Christ, not the gifts He has bestowed on me. I wasn't able to continue worshipping on the worship team, but I had won the battle with my arm, and the fight was not over. Every time the church doors were opened, I would worship with both arms lifted high as I whispered songs from my heart to my Restorer. As I continued to praise Him through my storm, the Holy Spirit used one of my doctors to share information leading to a decision that helped restore my voice. I was told it would be at least a year if it did come back, but God restored it within a few months. I remember it was on Mother's Day when I returned to ministering with my husband as he led worship. God gave me the best gift that year!

The battles aren't ours when we walk with our Savior. I knew there was so much more that God had in store for my life, and He wasn't finished with me yet. The devil knew this too and was trying to take me out. With a very bleak prognosis, God came out the victor and conquered the death sentence for me! I am forever grateful for the battles and the testimonies I have to share from that time of my life. God is so much bigger than our circumstances and will prove it to us if we continue to fight like warriors and give Him honor and praise in the process. Surround yourself with His presence; that is your greatest weapon.

I know God didn't bring me through that storm for nothing. There is more, and I am listening. Position yourself to hear God's voice as you read on.

CHAPTER 1

Worry

Is It God or Is It Me?

"For I know the plans I have for you," declares the LORD, *"plans to prosper you and not to harm you, plans to give you hope and a future."*

—Jeremiah 29:11 (NIV)

We all have heard the verse. We have seen it posted on wall decorations, jewelry, and even in our churches. He knows what our future holds; He has already provided the blueprint for us. The Message version of this verse states, "I know what I'm doing. I have it all planned out—plans to take care of you, not abandon you, plans to give you the future you hope for." Still, knowing His Word and believing it for yourself is another thing.

There are many scriptures that give us guidance. One of God's commands for us is to "hide His word in our heart" (Psalm 119:11) and to use it "as a light for our path" (Psalm 119:105) as well as respect it as "the perfect law that gives freedom" (James 1:25 NIV). If we don't do this, James 1:23 states it is like looking at ourselves into a mirror and then walking away and forgetting immediately what we look like. James goes on to state that IF we look at His Word and continue in it, not forgetting what we have heard but acting on it, we will be blessed. Why wouldn't we? He has plans and blessings for us!

Now the harder part: how do you know that what you are hearing, feeling, dreaming about is God's plan and purpose for you? There were so many thoughts that always haunted me: *What if this is just me designing this grand plan? What if I am being pompous? I mean…who's to know, right? The devil comes like a roaring lion and definitely will read my mail to know how to get to me. He could be "dangling a carrot," and I would be stupid enough to chomp, or would I?*

Well, I believe that after many years of living in denial, uncertainty, and disobedience, I can help answer that question.

The answer is really simple, but we have to go to God's Word to find it. Christians get all caught up in worrying if they are good enough for God to use in a large capacity. It is easier for us to stay in a comfortable position that comes easily to us. We all have God-given talents and a calling on our lives to use them. How we will use them is very vague. The answer is—drumroll, please—if we are using God's Word as a light for our path, hiding His promises in our heart and living according to His laws and blueprints, then what we are hearing is God's voice. The Word challenges us to live righteously.

Psalm 5:12 states, "The Lord blesses the righteous, and He surrounds them with favor." Perfection is not the mandate, just willingness to admit the wrongs and then be repentant. Living righteously means to choose to live a life free of sin. You would be choosing to follow Paul's example and "die daily" to yourself so that the Holy Spirit can lead the way. Once you accept Christ as your Savior and believe in Him, you are His; you are a part of His family.

Galatians 5:24–25 (KJV) states, "And they that are Christ's have crucified the flesh with the affections and lusts. If we live in the Spirit, let us also walk in the Spirit." As believers in Christ, we have to crucify our passions and the desires of our sinful nature by nailing them to the cross so we can clearly hear to follow the Spirit's leading.

If you want to know if it is your idea or God's, you will have to do this daily. You will know without a doubt if you are living accordingly by aligning yourself with God's Word. You cannot align yourself with the Word if you aren't studying it daily to know it.

Only then will you see the favor of God surround you and the plan for your life, the blueprint, begin to unfold before you.

God won't allow you to see the next season of your life if you have not conquered the current battle. We move forward with every victory in our lives. Each step forward allows us to see God's plan a little more clearly.

I know, eye-opening, right? God has an expected future for each of us; as the New King James Version states, He has given us His Word as a guide to build our right relationship with Him. He has given it to us as a road map on how to live a holy life. If we are doing that faithfully, then our relationship with Him will be so close that there will not be a doubt as to whether it is God or just us.

As I stated previously, I have lived in disobedience for years. You ask, "How is that disobedience if you didn't know?" Well, let me explain. I knew the Scripture, and I knew in my mind all the right things to say and do as a Christian, but my heart was not aligned with my mind.

The first chapter of James explains clearly what I was doing. I was hearing the Word but not obeying it. I was going through the motions of what I knew but not acting on it. Sadly, it took many years of heartache and pain for me to get it aligned, but I would have it no other way.

You see, I was once a singer and a member of a worship team, but now I am a worshipper (whether all go with me…still, I will follow Christ). Once I decided to worship God as the Bible instructs for me to do and to do it unashamedly, I could hear His voice in worship. If I believe with all that is in my heart, mind, and spirit that God knows the plans that are to prosper me, AND if I live according to His Word, walking in a relationship with Him, then there is no doubt that it is God talking to me.

You see, the Holy Spirit gives you discernment through your relationship with Him. Hebrews 4:12 states that the Word of God is alive and active. It goes on to say that it judges the thoughts and attitudes of the heart. God knows you, and He will guide you into His plan for you. You have to be obedient and faithful to His Word.

God knows our needs and our weaknesses too. He knew I needed to know without a doubt that this book was His design and not mine. He knew that I was weak in my thoughts as I took steps to begin, but He confirmed through fellow Christians that what I was writing wasn't just me but a vessel being led by Him. It was an amazing feeling as things began to unfold. He knows exactly what we need.

If you are struggling with knowing if it's you or God, then pray this prayer and follow these steps to see what God's blueprint is for your life.

Prayer

Dear God, help me to actively be seeking Your plans for my life. Show me my heart's true intentions as I seek You. Help me to lay aside any thoughts of doubt or inability and to believe what Your Word says. Help me to live out Your Word daily, and when life gets tough, help me to stand on Your promises. Help me to hide Your Word in my heart, to use it as a guide for my life and to honor it as the law of freedom for Your purpose to be fulfilled within me. I pray this in Your great name, Jesus. Amen.

Reflection

1. Am I talking with God daily?
2. Do I pray for discernment?
3. Am I faithful to hide His Word in my heart and not just my head?
4. Do I allow God to show me what He wants for me, or do I go about my day doing the same old stuff until Sunday?

Reflection Notes

____

____

____

____

____

____

If you cannot honestly answer that you have been obedient and not defiant in your relationship with God, I pray you make the decision to TRULY follow Him with all of you—not just your mind but your body and spirit as well.

CHAPTER 2

The Unknown

Pick Up Your Cross and Follow Me

Then Jesus told his disciples, "If anyone would come after me, let him deny himself and take up his cross and follow me. For whoever would save his life will lose it, but whoever loses his life for my sake will find it."

—Matthew 16:24–25 (KJV)

Have you ever seen someone walking down the road pulling a big wooden cross on wheels? I have. I have thought to myself about the sacrifice that person is making for Christ as they trek across the country.

Then I begin to question, *Do I have to carry a physical cross as I minister?* Absolutely not. *What about the people who do? Is that truly doing ministry, and would that mean mine is half-hearted?* Absolutely not. God has ordained each one of His children's steps. Everyone has their own unique calling within God's kingdom.

As followers of Christ, we cannot do everything on our own. All the body of Christ is needed to get His Word out and His work complete. In 1 Corinthians 12, the Bible speaks about the body of Christ and how it is one body with many parts. Each part is needed and does not work well without the other parts. One way you could look at it is this; try to follow along.

A post by Mike Battista, a staff scientist at Cambridge Brain Sciences, shares a quote from a page written by Mike Davis, who investigates for CBS Medical Research Council on how the brain processes language: "It deosn't mttaer in waht oredr the ltteers in a wrod are, the olny iprmoetnt tihng is taht the frist and lsat ltteer be at the rghit pclae."

Wtih the bdoy of Csihrt, it is the smae. All the prtas may be trhee, but it is a lot eisaer to wrok for Csrhit wehn tnighs are in aglnimnet or in odrer.

You can do things a lot easier when it is being done the way it was intended. We, as humans, look at things as a whole. We do not think about all the individuals it takes to make up the body of Christ until something is lacking or someone isn't doing their part.

The Message interpretation of these verses reads this way:

> Then Jesus went to work on his disciples. "Anyone who intends to come with me has to let me lead. You're not in the driver's seat; I am. Don't run from suffering; embrace it. Follow me and I'll show you how. Self-help is no help at all. Self-sacrifice is the way, my way, to finding yourself, your true self."

I love it! Now I know where my parents got those sayings like "My way or the highway." Jesus is telling us that to follow Him means we are not just doing things for Him but also doing them His way. Joseph Kennedy stated, "When the going gets tough, the tough get going." Jesus is saying this by telling us to embrace the suffering. We can positive-talk ourselves only so far through hardships because we are not strong enough without Him. We have to lay down our lives, our own will, into His hands to be able to find His way.

That's the big thing I've been having to deal with. It is HIS WAY, not just HIS WILL. I have been willing to lay down my cross and pick up His for whatever He has next for me, but I don't know the next step. So what do I do?

I have to be faithful and continue to follow His will and pray for Him to have His way. I have to prayerfully take steps. Honestly, I struggle, just like many of you, with doing daily what I know it takes to follow His will. It is so much easier to take the path of the "busy life." *I am too tired to get up early and write. I work all day and then am mom and wife all evening. God knows my heart, and that is what counts. God doesn't expect me to do this every day.*

Well, when I started accepting those ideas, I stopped writing for two months! It is so easy to get busy with life, and that is not denying ourselves.

We have a choice to choose this day whom we will serve, and then we have a choice to serve Him or to talk about it. Each choice we make leads to another.

Are you following Him and His way for your life? If you do not know what that is yet, are you seeking Him daily to build the relationship with Him so you can hear His voice speaking to you? The body of Christ needs you. You read it right; God needs you to be the part of the body that He intended for you to be. We all have an ordained part. Unless you deny your way and seek His way, you may never fully be in alignment with Him to complete His purpose for your life. Do I think that is sin? No. I just believe God will raise up another to complete what is needed. Wouldn't you rather work in your capacity that God ordained you to be?

Just think of the world and how great it would be if we all would do as Matthew 16:24–25 says. Every messed-up thing would go back into order. We can't fix this world, but we can do our part with God as our guide. We need each other, but we have to have God first guiding us. Things will fall into place easier when we do what He has intended for us, and we are all involved. It takes all of us doing our part.

If you are struggling with laying it down and following God, then pray this prayer and follow these steps to see what God's blueprint is for your life.

Prayer

Dear God, help me to actively be seeking not only Your will but also Your way for my life. Show me how to find You in my daily life. Help me to lay aside any thoughts of self-help or defeat and to believe You're the only way for me to find my true self.

Help me to let You lead my life, and when life gets tough, help me to stand and embrace it. Help me to seek You daily, remind me to find Your guidance for my life, and help me to see and know what my part is in the kingdom. I pray this in Your great name, Jesus. Amen.

Reflection

1. Am I talking with God daily specifically for my purpose?
2. Do I pray for His will and way?
3. Am I faithful to lay aside my own agenda and pick up His?
4. Do I trust and follow God each day or just when I think it is necessary?

Reflection Notes

____

____

____

____

____

____

____

If you feel lost and without purpose, I challenge you to read God's promises daily and apply them to your life. If you have accepted Jesus, then you have to accept all of Him (He is the Word) and not just with your mind. He wants your will and your way so He can give you His.

Talk to God; when we call, He answers. The next choice is to listen and obey.

CHAPTER 3

Fear and Unworthiness

Beatitudes

You are blessed.

—Matthew 5

Most everyone has, at some point, read or been taught the Beatitudes from the Bible. Many have learned a little song in Sunday school or memorized them for Bible Quiz. We know what the Word says; the problem is that we were so young and oblivious to the meaning and promise to us that we now tend to skim over it as adults. We think we already know that story, so why read it again?

Several years ago, I was lying in bed and couldn't sleep. I was praying for God to speak to me again. I was desperate for a fresh word or direction from the Lord. As I lay there, all I saw in my mind's eye was the word *Beatitude*. With encouragement of receiving a "word," I pondered what that meant. I, of course, didn't think too deeply upon it. I thought, *Hey, maybe God is giving me something to make money with and bless my family financially.*

So I looked it up online and found out that He had already blessed someone else with that idea. *Hmmm?* I was stumped. I got out the Bible and read the King James Version that we all know from our childhood. Still nothing. I prayed for understanding and for more details, and I just got a blank slate. Nothing new plopped into my mind. I decided to write it down and come back to it later. I thought maybe God was going to add to it after I slept.

He didn't. For several years, I had a page in my notes that only read the word *Beatitudes*. What was I supposed to do with that? When God started convicting me to pick up my cross and follow Him instead of just sitting around holding my cross, I started going through the notes I had written over the years. As I came across the *Beatitudes* note, I pondered it for a split second and then deleted it. I thought that must have been me and not God.

A few weeks later, my pastor was preaching on—wait for it—"This Day Leads to That Day." I was ecstatic! My book was entitled *This Is the Day*. I was excited to see what he meant by it leading to "that day." This was not the first time that what God had been speaking to me was then preached from the pulpit. God had been giving me weekly confirmations of my writings. Don't we have an amazing God! That He would even take the time to reassure me that it was His thoughts and not mine blows my mind! He knows our weaknesses and is our strength when we are in doubt. He loves us more than even our earthly father.

I know that is so hard to imagine, but take a moment and think about those words. Wow! Anyway, as the pastor began to preach, he read from Matthew 5, where it talks about how everyone came because they had heard of Jesus's healing power and life-changing power. He then began to read the Beatitudes. What! Again, God was speaking to me. I thought, *No, I deleted it!*

Although I had read, skimmingly, over the Beatitudes many times using different versions of the Bible, it was different that Sunday. My eyes were opened to the true meanings, the promises. I became weepy realizing just how much God loves us and wants to bless us. He said, "Be blessed…under His protection and favor." I knew that was for me.

God knows our thoughts. I had been pondering God's favor over my life and the protection He had given me over the years while He waited for me to be obedient. Our pastor reminded us that being healed doesn't mean that we will never get sick again. I knew this, but I was reassured by knowing He blesses us with protection and favor. The key is the rest of the scripture.

Let's look at the Message version together. Matthew 5:1–12 states,

> When Jesus saw his ministry drawing huge crowds, he climbed a hillside. Those who were apprenticed to him, the committed, climbed with him. Arriving at a quiet place, he sat down and taught his climbing companions. This is what he said:…

Let's pause there for a moment. It stated that "those who were apprenticed to him, the committed" are whom he taught these things to. *Webster's* definition of apprentice is (a) "one bound by indenture (contract) to serve another for a prescribed period with a view to learning an art or trade" and (b) "one who is learning by practical experience under skilled workers a trade, art, or calling—a carpenter's apprentice."

Did you catch that? A person bound to serve another for a prescribed period with the view of learning the calling: a carpenter's apprentice. See, I read that as this: Jesus is the carpenter who is teaching us His ways as we walk in our calling to follow Him.

He spoke these things to them because they were the ones who needed to hear His promises for the sacrifices they were making in their lives to follow Him. It was to help them realize they were walking in His will no matter what happens along that journey.

This just tells us that things are still going to happen to us even though we are followers of Christ. We aren't in a glass bubble that can't be penetrated. We will be under attack throughout the journey, but God has many promises for His committed apprentices.

Let's look at those blessings in parallel with how we "know" them (KJV) and how God intends for us to "know" them (MSG):

> Blessed are the poor in spirit: for theirs is the kingdom of heaven. (Matthew 5:3 KJV)

> You're blessed when you're at the end of your rope. With less of you, there is more of God and his rule. (Matthew 5:3 MSG)

When you are feeling you are at the end of your rope in ministry or even in life, that is when God can truly show you what He has for you. I felt so complacent and almost as if my life had plateaued. I knew there was something more. I began praying for Him to speak to me and promised to respond if He would. He had room to talk where I could hear since I decided to lay down my negative thoughts and take on the desperation for more.

> Blessed are they that mourn: for they shall be comforted. (Matthew 5:4 KJV)

> You're blessed when you feel you've lost what is most dear to you. Only then can you be embraced by the One most dear to you. (Matthew 5:4 MSG)

God will be your comfort when you feel like everything around you is caving in. Those nights you lie awake crying out to God about your circumstances, the Holy Spirit is there to comfort you. When you feel you are doing everything God has asked of you and you are suffering for it, just remember, He has not left you. To suffer is Christ in you! Push on as you follow Him faithfully.

> Blessed are the meek: for they shall inherit the earth. (Matthew 5:5 KJV)

> You're blessed when you're content with just who you are—no more, no less. That's the moment you find yourselves proud owners of everything that can't be bought. (Matthew 5:5 MSG)

When you are walking out what you believe in your heart is God's calling for you, you will feel proud and powerful. He is your strength. I can't buy anything that gives me the peace and the wonderful feeling of doing something for Christ. It is priceless!

> Blessed are they which do hunger and thirst after righteousness: for they shall be filled. (Matthew 5:6 KJV)

> You're blessed when you've worked up a good appetite for God. He's food and drink in the best meal you'll ever eat. (Matthew 5:6 MSG)

As you are taking the steps that God has ordained for you, your desire for more of Him becomes ever present in your life. You will want to hear more and know more. You will be filled with knowledge and truth because you are now listening as He speaks to you. Each word I type causes me to want to sit at the computer all day long just to see what else God is going to speak to me. I long for the next enlightenment of His Word for my life!

> Blessed are the merciful: for they shall obtain mercy. (Matthew 5:7 KJV)

> You're blessed when you care. At the moment of being "care-full," you find yourselves cared for. (Matthew 5:7 MSG)

As your heart softens to God's voice, you will find yourself becoming more merciful to those around you. God shows us mercy as our heart is tender to His will and way. I have seen this in my life. When I was in need of prayer and I prayed for someone else specifically with the fervency I would want someone praying for me, I ended up with MY healing!

> Blessed are the pure in heart: for they shall see God. (Matthew 5:8 KJV)

> You're blessed when you get your inside world—your mind and heart—put right. Then you can see God in the outside world. (Matthew 5:8 MSG)

As you follow Christ, you will see that He is changing not only the way you think and feel but also everything around you; it will look different. You will begin to see things as God sees them. Your heart will feel with the compassion that God has for this world. You will look at the world and all the people differently. His mercy will be extended through your actions.

> Blessed are the peacemakers: for they shall be called the children of God. (Matthew 5:9 KJV)

> You're blessed when you can show people how to cooperate instead of compete or fight. That's when you discover who you really are, and your place in God's family. (Matthew 5:9 MSG)

As a follower of Christ, when you lay aside your own agenda and take on His, you will be able to take the compassion you have from seeing with His eyes and help others. When you work in the church, you see and often hear about the battles of our brothers and sisters in Christ. God will lead them to you because you have been called to be the peacemaker. All families have the peacemaker—that person who always calms the others and helps them see things from all vantage points.

As you are following God and learning from His Word, you will be able to speak life into each situation. When peace comes for that situation, you will have a great big smile on your face and an overwhelming joy in your heart, knowing that you are doing your part in the family.

> Blessed are they which are persecuted for righteousness' sake: for theirs is the kingdom of heaven. (Matthew 5:10 KJV)

> You're blessed when your commitment to God provokes persecution. The persecution drives you even deeper into God's kingdom. (Matthew 5:10 MSG)

When you are going after God and everything feels right but all of a sudden another person says something that causes you to doubt your intentions or worth, what do you do? You can choose to give up, become defensive, or you can press on and not allow your thoughts or emotions to be controlled by others. Let those things cause you to seek God more and to be confident in your walk with Him.

> Blessed are ye, when men shall revile you, and persecute you, and shall say all manner of evil against you falsely, for my sake.
>
> Rejoice, and be exceeding glad: for great is your reward in heaven: for so persecuted they the prophets which were before you. (Matthew 5:11–12 KJV)

> Not only that—count yourselves blessed every time people put you down or throw you out or

speak lies about you to discredit me. What it means is that the truth is too close for comfort and they are uncomfortable. You can be glad when that happens—give a cheer, even!—for though they don't like it, I do! And all heaven applauds. And know that you are in good company. My prophets and witnesses have always gotten into this kind of trouble. (Matthew 5:11–12 MSG)

You are going to have setbacks, trials, and even torment when doing what God has asked you to do. If you don't have battles, then you are doing something wrong because the enemy isn't going to let us further God's kingdom without a fight. Fighting with the Word of God and pressing on will make you stronger as a warrior for Christ. Look at Job! No matter his trial, he pressed on and continued to trust God.

The Beatitudes cause me to be in awe, to ponder His love and care for His children. Reflecting on all His promises of blessings as we follow Him just seems to make it so much easier. No matter what, if we see things through His eyes, we will see that we are blessed beyond measure. I will continue to praise Him through the storms so my That Day comes with promise.

If you are struggling with being an apprentice of Christ, pray this prayer as often as you need until you are able to walk as an apprentice for Christ.

Prayer

Dear God, I know that I am weak. Yet in my weakness, You are strong. Right now, I do not feel Your strength, but I see it in You. I need it. I want to be Your apprentice. I don't want to preach it, teach it, sing about it, or write about it without living it. Help me to practice what I believe. Help my mind, heart, and actions align to apprenticeship. Help me to walk in my blessings even in the midst of the hardest times. Help me to press on and not lie down in the fight when it gets tough. I desperately need You to remind me daily that I am blessed as I see with Your eyes. I pray all this in Your name, Jesus. Amen.

Reflection

1. What is it He is calling you to do?
2. What is it that is holding you back from being an apprentice of Christ?
3. Are you willing to sacrifice for Christ?

Reflection Notes

____

____

____

____

____

____

If you haven't been walking in your blessings, I encourage you to read the Beatitudes each day until you believe God's promises are true for you. Take a step of faith, align your heart and mind with His Word, and become a follower "this" day to have promise for "that" great day!

CHAPTER 4

Blockades

Warrior for God

*Put on the whole armour of God, that ye may be
able to stand against the wiles of the devil.*

—Ephesians 6:11 (KJV)

Wiles of the devil? The online version of *Merriam-Webster*'s dictionary defines *wiles* as "a trick or stratagem intended to ensnare or deceive" and also "a beguiling or playful trick." God knew in advance that we were going to be tricked, tempted, or trapped in situations that were not for our benefit. *Why would God allow things like this to happen to us?* Now wait a minute! We just decided to lay down our lives, fearlessly step out, and follow Him.

It says in His Word that He is our protector and that He wants to prosper us as His children. That seems very hard to believe when we are in the middle of hearing that we need triple bypass surgery and the complications and risks are high, or our child has just been diagnosed with a terminal disease. How do we follow Him with all the blockades that come our way?

Well, if we are going to use God's Word for all the good stuff, we also have to read the rest of it. This is the reason it is so important to read not just the inspiring scriptures on Facebook or your "verse of the day" as your daily time with Christ. Those are great for encouraging words, but you have to go deeper to bring depth to your relationship and strength to your faith.

When you have others you are responsible for, you don't just teach about the good things but also let them know the hardships that could arise as well and how to deal with them. Like driving. There are many benefits to getting your license, but many precautions have to be learned as well. Our heavenly Father does the same for you; God's Word gives you the tools to succeed through good and bad times.

There are also life stories written in the Bible that are testimonies for you to read and learn from. You have one or even many to share with those around you that either you have experienced firsthand or someone has shared with you. Remember them out loud for others to experience God's miraculous works during the bad or tough times.

I used to teach students with emotional disturbances who had extremely traumatic lives. I, without bringing up God, had to help them learn that life can be good for them too and there are good people out there. I tried to help them regulate their emotions by teaching them strategies that would be tools in their lives to help them succeed emotionally.

There are a lot of "if-thens" in life, good and bad. These are all consequences of our choices of action. I taught the students that our thoughts create our feelings, which we then act upon. They learned there were tools we all have to use on a daily, sometimes hourly, basis: coping strategies. This is very real in everyone's life. It is so hard to stop and think about the best choice in the heat of the moment, whether despair and heartache or rage and retaliation. To be able to do this, we have to learn more about it, and we have to practice making those right choices. God has given us all the tools. We just have to apply them to our lives.

God has given us an instruction manual: the Bible. We have to read it to learn from others' accounts and from the commands and promises that are mapped out for all who believe. When we are given devastating news, we have to think about our spiritual "if-thens." If we have read and believe God's Word to be true, if we pray, if we turn from our sins, if we apply His Word in our lives, if we step into our calling and follow Him, then we will have all the promises mapped out for us. We will be able to stand for everything tossed our way. The scripture verse from the Message version reads like this: "So take everything the Master has set out for you, well-made weapons of the best materials. And put them to use so you will be able to stand up to everything the Devil throws your way."

You may ask, "What are the well-made weapons that he has set out for me?" I am so glad you asked. You see, if you take ALL his Word and apply it to your life, then you will be able to see how you were made for war. You were given the tools and strategies to fight the enemy from any angle. You are a warrior.

If you were to read on in Ephesians chapter 6 (KJV), you would find the description of the armor you have been given to fight all your battles and to assist others in theirs. Let's look at it:

> For we wrestle not against flesh and blood, but against principalities, against powers, against the rulers of the darkness of this world, against spiritual wickedness in high places. Wherefore take unto you the whole armour of God, that ye may be able to withstand in the evil day, and having done all, to stand. Stand therefore, having your loins girt about with truth, and having on the breastplate of righteousness; And your feet shod with the preparation of the gospel of peace; Above all, taking the shield of faith, wherewith ye shall be able to quench all the fiery darts of the wicked. And take the helmet of salvation, and the sword of the Spirit, which is the word of God: Praying always with all prayer and supplication in the Spirit, and watching thereunto with

all perseverance and supplication for all saints.
(Ephesians 6:12–18 KJV)

For those who need that put in our everyday vernacular, the Message version of the Bible reads like this:

> This is no afternoon athletic contest that we'll walk away from and forget about in a couple of hours. This is for keeps, a life-or-death fight to the finish against the Devil and all his angels. Be prepared. You're up against far more than you can handle on your own. Take all the help you can get, every weapon God has issued, so that when it's all over but the shouting you'll still be on your feet. Truth, righteousness, peace, faith, and salvation are more than words. Learn how to apply them. You'll need them throughout your life. God's Word is an indispensable weapon. In the same way, prayer is essential in this ongoing warfare. Pray hard and long. Pray for your brothers and sisters. Keep your eyes open. Keep each other's spirits up so that no one falls behind or drops out. (Ephesians 6:12–18 MSG)

I have found that when I am going through a storm, I get through it faster and without doubt if I am not focused on the problem but on hearing from the Lord. Prayer is essential in battle. I was going through cancer, yet my prayers were for my family, my sister (who was going through a divorce), our church (where we had just become worship pastors), and my previous pastor's wife (who had been in a traumatic car accident). I had to keep warring for everyone around me. I had to be in His presence daily to feel His healing over my life. I hid His Word in my heart. When I would go in for tests or treatments, I would praise Him during the drive to the facility. While lying in a machine as it roared around me, I would listen to the local

Christian radio station and quote His Word. His Word is our sword for battle! I would not be "anxious about anything."

Philippians 4:6 states, "Don't fret or worry. Instead of worrying, pray. Let petitions and praises shape your worries into prayers, letting God know your concerns. Before you know it, a sense of God's wholeness, everything coming together for good, will come and settle you down."

I am so grateful to report that God has never failed me. He sees past my faults of doubt and fear and meets my needs. He will do the same for you! When the bumps and potholes get in your way, when the enemy is attacking, put on your armor!

I am sure many of you have faced challenges that seemed too much to bear. Don't take your helmet off and lay your sword down. You need all the armor that God has provided to beat the devil at his schemes. Show him what you are made of! Verbally put on your armor daily, and the warrior within you will rise up.

If you are struggling with a tidal wave of fear or if it seems like there are roadblocks in every direction, pray this prayer with me and then reflect on your situation. God knows your every situation, and that doesn't change His calling on your life. Psalm 46:1–3 states that God is our refuge and strength, an ever-present help in trouble. It only adds to the testimony you will have.

Prayer

Dear God, hear my cry this day to see Your light in my situation and circumstances. Things seem bleak to me right now, and there doesn't seem to be a window or door of escape. Please help me to listen to hide Your words in my heart daily so I can continue to fight this battle.

I am NOT defeated. I am a child of the King; You go before me and prepare a way when there seems to be no way. You have equipped me with armor to face every battle. You have a calling and purpose for my life greater than I can ever fathom, and I am fighting to increase my testimony for Your glory. I am fighting to put the devil in his place—under my feet!

Thank You for Your guidance and direction. Thank You for strength in each moment of my day. Thank You for restoring my strength and energy as I go to battle for what You have in store for my life. Find me in Your favor, Lord, and heal my land. Amen.

Reflection

1. Call it out. Name the challenge you are facing that seems to be blocking the calling on your life.
2. Are you warring for what God has birthed inside of you in spite of your circumstances? Speak to the mountain to move; God's not done with you. Wear your armor of Christ daily, and defeat the enemy with God's Word.
3. Are you carrying your sword?

Reflection Notes

____

____

____

____

____

____

Find a scripture that you can cling to. Write it on your mirror so you can see it daily. Put notes on the refrigerator, in the bathroom, or at your bedside with God's words. Set random alarms on your phone to go off with scripture verses as the name of the alarm that pops up. Make a key chain of flip-card scripture to be your go-to in times of weakness. You have the tools; use them to war and to strengthen the warrior inside you.

So many more testimonies will develop as you win and squash the devil's schemes against you and accept God's calling on your life. The devil wants nothing more than to have you feel defeated so you stop pushing on toward the calling God has for you.

CHAPTER 5

Wounded while in Battle

Band-Aids

A cheerful heart is good medicine, but a
crushed spirit dries up the bones.

—Proverbs 17:22 (NIV)

It is an awesome feeling when you have finally heard the direction for God's calling in your life, put on the armor that He provided, and begun to walk out in faith headed toward "that day." Your heart is so light, and you feel so at peace.

You carry yourself with a joyful disposition. As you go about your days, you see God's hand in so many things as they unfold. There are times, as you are confidently walking out your calling, battles will come along that you feel completely prepared for. You are wearing your spiritual armor, and your communication with God hasn't missed a beat, but you get wounded. This hurts most when you weren't expecting it to come, and it comes from someone close. You try to talk yourself through to healing by telling yourself they didn't mean it or some justifiable excuse, but every time you see them, the hurt rises within you, and you try to avoid them.

When you're hurting because there is something or someone who has cut you deeply, only Christ can heal your broken heart and broken mind. Only our Savior can fix the broken pieces by putting them back together and molding the clay back into His original creation.

If you do not apply God's Word to help mend and heal your brokenness, the wounds fester and infection sets in. Bitterness, low self-worth, anger, or even disdain begins to consume your thoughts. As that infects your spirit, it begins to kill your desire to continue the calling and purpose you feel in your life. You begin to lack drive and motivation in the ministries you already are involved in because you are angry, are sulking, or have just given up. The wound isn't healing. You begin to question God; how could He let this happen? Everything was going great, and now this! To us, it seems like everything's on hold, but God expects us to use the armor, not just wear it.

I was cutting a chunk of pepperoni one day, and I accidentally cut into my finger. It wouldn't stop bleeding. I put a Band-Aid on it, and when I thought it was better, I took it off. While trying to go about my normal day, I would hit my finger on things or catch it on clothes, and it would begin bleeding all over again. I would start the cycle again: Band-Aid, remove it, catch or hit it on something, and bleed again. I decided I needed to put a bigger Band-Aid on it and add some extra wrapping. I needed to keep it covered until it was totally mended. That was the only way to protect the wound.

When you are hurt, you can listen to a sermon and say a prayer that is focused on your needs, and at that moment, you feel better. You come away with a sense of healing and knowing that God has got this. You feel empowered again to move forward. It's like a Band-Aid for your soul and mind.

However, the problem is that you go right back into your normal routine of life, and someone or something will rub you the wrong way or catch you off guard, and you are wounded again. You forgot to apply the medicine. You may be studying God's Word, but even in the tough times, you have to apply it to your life. If you don't, then you cannot heal, and you let your wounds fester.

Your relationships begin to fall apart. You begin avoiding people who have hurt you. If they worked in ministry with you, you may begin stepping away from ministering with them. Eventually, you will find excuses not to go to church, you will start talking about the situation in a manner to hurt the other party, and you will finally become hard-hearted.

You see, we are like glass. We may be beautiful on the outside, but we get cracked, chipped, and even broken. The great reality is that we can be softened and reformed by getting in the fire of God. It takes sacrificing our will of wanting to be upset or wallowing in our hurt to find our healing. The fire is at the altar of our sacrifice.

Even David, a man after God's own heart, wrote of the pain and wounds he had from others' words. Psalm 69 is a song he wrote describing his situation. He is hurting, looking for God in the midst of the situation. He asks God to be his vengeance. He ends with praising God. David wrote in verse 30 (NIV), "I will praise God's name in song and glorify him with thanksgiving." Praising God, talking with God—that is the key to healing inside and out.

God's Word is truth, and if you apply it to every situation, you can be healed by your belief: faith. The answer to all you are going through is in the Bible. A sermon, a devotion, a worship song, a conversation with a spiritually mature brother or sister in Christ all help and are part of the healing process. Laying it down at Jesus's feet daily and speaking what is true over your life is where you find complete healing. Fast and pray for your mind to be mended and your heart to be healed. Give it to God like David did so you may have joy again.

As Proverbs 17:22 (ESV) states, "a joyful heart is good medicine, but a crushed spirit dries up the bones." Speak to those bones to live again! Let God breathe life into you again so that you may continue on your God journey to "that day." You have to continue to pursue God even when you have been hurt by someone. God will show you the mending process for your situation, and as you heal, He has given you another testimony for your ministry to others.

Prayer

God, my heart is heavy, and I feel plowed over. I knew life was going to get tough when I chose to step out for Your will in my life. I knew the devil was going to try to deter me. I just wasn't ready for this. Help me; heal my heart. I am hurting. I don't want to lose sight of "that day." I can't let the devil win and steal my joy.

Please, God, restore unto me the joy of my salvation and renew a right spirit within me. Help me to forgive like I have been forgiven. Help me to hear Your voice daily and see You in the little things of my life, especially when I feel overwhelmed with sorrow. Let the song I need to hear play on the radio, let the sermons I hear help mend my wounds, and send the right spiritual encourager my way.

Set a hedge of protection around me as I heal, dear God. Help me to remember to apply Your Word to my life and situations. I praise You for caring for me. I praise You for restoring my joy and helping me to continue Your will. I love You, Lord. Amen.

Reflection

1. Have you been going along, doing what you know God has called you to do, and BAM, you were sidelined? Did you find healing, or did you suppress the pain?
2. God has called us to renew our minds. How can you do this with your situation?
3. What steps have you taken or can you take to help your healing process? Start with giving forgiveness.

Reflection Notes

Let God restore and heal your heart. If you haven't been side-lined, be prepared because you will be. If you are warring, wounds are going to happen. If you are fighting for Christ, the enemy is stirring up things to find your weakness. Be strong in Christ, and keep on that armor!

CHAPTER 6

Transformation

Do not be conformed to this world, but be transformed by the renewal of your mind, that by testing you may discern what is the will of God, what is good and acceptable and perfect.

—Romans 12:2 (ESV)

I don't have to tell you that this journey is going to be long and hard. If you want being a follower of Christ to be easy, then you aren't really following Him. Following Him is a movement. You have to get up and go. There are steps to take, a walk to walk. We will stumble along the way; we may even get weary. Just getting saved and living with your salvation is an option, but that is not God's intention. He has called us all to go and compel others to Christ.

Mark 16:15 says that we are to go into all the world. Every person is created to do their part. You are destined for greatness in Christ! You just have to follow Him to find out your direction. You have to pray and listen for His voice. You have to get in His fire and get molded into His likeness. You have to take the time and read His Word; then apply it to all your situations. You will have many. Being molded, transformed, and renewed into believing you are whom God says you are a process of burning away chaff, breaking chains that have been holding you back (possibly for years), and learning to fix your eyes on His face. Seeking God's face will help you easily find His will.

Many times, there are things in our lives that are blocking our paths and we are oblivious to them. These are things in our lives that we have buried or justified to be acceptable. We have to pray for God to shine light on those things within our lives that need to be dealt with so we can continue our movement of following His call. This is the light shining on our shadows. We have to want His presence in our lives to drive out the darkness that lurks to take us off the path.

As we draw near to God, He will draw near to us. James 4:7 states this, but we need to remember the rest of the context. Let's look at the Message translation:

> So let God work His will in you. Yell a loud "no" to the Devil and watch him make himself scarce. Say a quiet "yes" to God and He'll be there in no time. Quit dabbling in sin. Purify your inner life. Quit playing the field. Hit bottom, and cry your eyes out. The fun and games are over. Get serious, really serious. Get down on your knees before the Master; it's the only way you'll get on your feet. (James 4:7–10 MSG)

There will never be transformation without revelation. There is no fence to ride when following Christ and walking in your purpose. Things have to die to begin the transformation. To begin the transition, you have to terminate selfishness and selfish ambitions. You have to eliminate anything in the way of pursuing Him.

The English Standard Version of James 1:12 states, "Blessed is the man who remains steadfast under trial, for when he has stood the test he will receive the crown of life, which God has promised to those who love him." It may hurt as you make permanent changes to your life, but that is the only way you can get moving again.

There is a billboard in our area of a realtor sitting on some luggage in front of a house with a realtor sign in the yard. The slogan says, "Pack your bags, and I'll do the rest." That is pretty sweet if someone is going to do all that for you, but then I realized that the packing is the hardest part. You have to figure out what to keep, what to throw out, give away, dust off and pack, and what you can sell. It is such a grueling process, but until you are done, you cannot enjoy your next dwelling place.

In your life, as you are desiring to transform into what God wants you to be, you have to clean up so you can move on. If you want to dwell in the secret place of the Almighty God, you have to make up your mind and begin the process. You know you have to keep your essentials—things that you know to be true and wholly pleasing to God. You have to dust off those areas of your life that you heard God's leading in but which you had set to the side while you "lived your life."

You must throw out the garbage in your life. These are things that you have held on to when you should have given them to God years ago. There may be some actual things you will have to burn to shake their hold off you. If there are idols in your life, things that you spend more time with than God, sell them. Use the money to further God's kingdom. Giving away things is just sharing what God is now doing in your life.

As you share about your transformation with others, you are holding yourself accountable to continuing your journey in God's will for your life. You are transforming and preparing to be used by God in a way you could not imagine. You have to clean and then pack your bags for the rest of the journey. God will do the rest if you are prepared and ready.

As you transform, you will be tried and tested, but remember, the fire has purified you. You are going to be able to know when it is God's will or yours. Your spiritual growth will become deeper and not just a mile long. There is so much more, and your hunger will continue to grow as you stay in His Word and continue to follow Him with your whole life.

Your transformation will make you remarkably changed in the eyes of others. I have struggles with this. My struggle was narrowed down to what others think about me. Well, as I am being transformed in Christ, I have learned that is an area in my life that needs to be put in the trash as I pack for my move. What others think of me does not matter, but pleasing my heavenly Father is the desire of my heart. If you are allowing your life to be transformed, then He will shine through you in every part of your life. People will see the power, favor, and anointing of God in the transformed version of you.

You have to renew your mind. I was praying in the prayer room at our church one Sunday between services. I kept hearing a strange noise, like something being dropped over and over. I looked around the room, and my eyes were drawn to the large windows. The sun was reflecting off the ice-covered tree branches, making them very bright to look at. I immediately walked over as I thought about how God's light is even so much brighter when lighting up the shadows in our lives.

All of a sudden, I found the source of the noise. The ice covered the leafless trees, and it was beautiful, but a transformation was happening. I watched the process for a while as God spoke to me. The transformation began as the sun heated the ice. The ice began to melt from the inside, and the water needed an escape. The ice became heavy from the weight of the water, and chunks of ice began to fall off.

In your life, you easily become cold and complacent at times. It takes the Son of God to "melt away the ice" to break off those things you have carried with you. That is a major step in your life when you allow the Son of God to change you from the inside out. All the things that have caused you to harden your heart and build walls begin to fall to the wayside.

There is more to the transformation. The sun doesn't just go away. The sun warms the leafless trees daily. Eventually, as they get warmer, fed, and watered, they begin to bloom and grow. It is a process. Now that you are daily exposing yourself to the Son of God, who is the Word, you will be nourished and will begin to grow. The fruits that you must carry will begin to bloom again. You will be transformed daily by God when you draw near to Him.

Prayer

God, I have begun this process of finding who I am in You. Please cleanse me, make me whole. Shine a light on every part of my life so that I can clean up, pack up, and let You move me to the place You have for me. Renew my mind, and help me to forgive and let go of things that may be holding me back. Convict me in areas that I have become complacent in so that I can be rejuvenated by Your light.

Help me to transform into the person You created me to be, and let Your power, favor, and anointing be my testimony of Your great work in my life. I love You, Lord, and want You more than the things of this world. Lead me so that my life reflects Your light. In Jesus's precious name. Amen.

Reflection

1. Am I a Christian following Christ, or am I just saved by His grace?
2. Is there anything in my life that is keeping me from being ready for God to "do the rest"?
3. What changes have I made that reflect the Son of God in my life? If none, what steps do I need to begin this next part of the cleanup?
4. What fruits of the Spirit are producing in your life, and what fruits are lacking? How can you grow those fruits in your life as you transform for Christ?

Reflection Notes

____

37

____

____

____

____

____

____

Let God transform you into becoming all that you are called to be for Him. I believe this is an ongoing process in our walk with Christ. As you pray, ask God to make you aware of what He wants you to do.

Fasting is an important part of hearing God's voice. Pray about how that should look in your life. God will reveal that to you as you draw near to Him and allow Him to nourish you for blooms and growth, deeply rooted in His Word. Seeking God's face (His presence) will help you easily find His will for your life. Being in His presence is your greatest weapon against all things that hinder your walk.

CHAPTER 7

I Am Who God Says I Am

*We demolish arguments and every pretension that sets
itself up against the knowledge of God, and we take
captive every thought to make it obedient to Christ.*

—2 Corinthians 10:5 (NIV)

For as he thinketh in his heart, so is he.

—Proverbs 23:7 (KJV)

The manuscript has been written; we just have to read it and apply it to our daily lives. One of the biggest battles I have is believing I can do more. I discovered along my journey that I cannot do more, but I can allow my life to be the vessel used by God. He can do more through me than I could fathom. I cannot imagine and do not pretend to know the depth of His calling on my life. I do, however, know what it takes to begin following Christ, to hear His voice, to discern between temptation and God's will, to heal from heartache, and to war for victory. I know the blessings He has promised me along this journey of transformation, going from this day to that day.

As I began writing this book, I faced many challenges. I would think to myself that I was too exhausted from my daily responsibilities to write. I would make myself feel better by telling myself that

I had all summer to work on it. The battle of the mind is so strong. Many Christian authors have written about that internal battle.

See, I knew that waiting until summer was not God's plan for me. God had already given me a summer, and I let myself get "too busy" to write. So many obstacles hindered me from doing what I knew I was supposed to do. I continued to push it off until "later." Until I took captive my negative and lackadaisical thoughts, I was bound from allowing God to "do the rest." There were many irons in the fire for me, and I felt overwhelmed about being able to do the things I felt God was calling me to do.

We are shaped daily by the thoughts we choose to allow into our hearts. Even the apostle Paul, in 1 Thessalonians, spoke of feeling hindered at times. We all get in this same position. Satan throws roadblocks up to stop us from fulfilling our calling.

One day, the verse from 2 Corinthians came to my mind while I was having a "Woe is me" thought. The Message version says it like this: "We use our powerful God-tools for smashing warped philosophies, tearing down barriers erected against the truth of God, fitting every loose thought and emotion and impulse into the structure of life shaped by Christ."

Whew, I just began reminding myself that God has greater things for me. I had to stop just telling others about how God has a plan for them and take action for my life. The first thing I had to do was to hold captive the loose thoughts that did not need to become a part of my daily lifestyle.

As I mentioned earlier in this book, our thoughts create our feelings, and then we act on them. We all have to make a choice, and after hiding God's Word in my heart over the years, I knew what actions I needed to take. I was to be obedient in order for the blessings of God to be in my life. I remembered the Word of God says that "as a man thinks, so he is." I changed my "stinking thinking" that day. I was made for more, and so are you.

Even when it seems too scary, you have to remember that it's God using us as a vessel. You have to remember His Word to carry you daily through the battle of life and against your flesh. War with the armor He has provided. There will be times in the journey that the task isn't as rewarding in the moment as you would like. There may be a waiting period! God may have to teach patience in the process. Every child of God is different, and He will show you the steps to take as you draw near and be obedient to follow Him.

God will wait for you to finish the first step of His plan before showing you the next step. Just remind yourself to do everything "without grumbling or arguing" (Philippians 2:14 NIV). You have to pray in the moment to help you walk in obedience. I have always said there are seasons of our lives, and we are given a lesson to learn in each. These lessons build our character and help us find our identity in Christ. We are who He says we are.

I tell my students that many people remember better and take things to heart more when it is said out loud. I have them test themselves. They will take a reading comprehension test first by reading silently. After a few weeks, I have them take a similar test but this time reading out loud so they can hear their voice. We then compare the scores, and in every situation so far, all the students scored higher on their comprehension and understanding of what they read when they had read it out loud to themselves. Now this, by no means, was a full study for peer-reviewed proof, but it definitely has opened my eyes as well as some students', who now choose to read out loud or have things read out loud to them.

It shows you that if you are focused on reading silently you still can have distractions. Although reading out loud can have distractions, those distractions are fewer if you are also listening to a voice. Having God's Word in your heart, knowing what He has promised His children, and believing you are who He says you are is a great thing. But you can comprehend and understand His Word more if you speak His Word over your life. We need to quote His Word and take captive our thoughts daily. We need to remind ourselves who He says we are. It takes courage and strength, but He formed us in our mother's womb already knowing His plans for us.

I am a free new creation adopted into the kingdom of God, saved by grace, and now alive in Christ and no longer a slave to sin or fear, now a branch on the vine to bear His fruit, now an heir of God in which I share in His suffering and also His glory, now an ambassador for Christ, now a citizen of heaven waiting for His return as I humbly do all things through Christ, Who gives me my strength.

Prayer

God, I am who You say I am. I was bought at a price and not just to sit around and wait for You to take me home to Glory. I want to know You more. I want to hear Your voice daily for me and my family. Help me to not just hide Your words in my heart but also speak them over my life and those of others. Help me to take captive every thought so that I can pursue You with the purest of heart and mind.

As I continue my steps toward Your next season for me, help me to remember who I truly am. Thank You, Lord, for having a plan for my life and giving me the opportunity to be Your vessel. I love You, Lord. Amen.

Reflection

1. Do I really believe with all my being that I am who God says I am? What thoughts do I need to hold captive or purge from my heart that are keeping me from believing God's Word to be true for me?

2. What steps can I take to begin speaking life and God's Word in my daily routine? Where will I begin? When will I begin?

3. Take time today to write out who God says you are, contradicting all the lies that have chained you down. You are good enough because you are His.

Reflective Notes

42

God has called you, has anointed you, has found favor with you, and is waiting for you to draw near. Take up your cross and follow Him. Wear the provided armor and war for your life as you become an ambassador for Him. God has many blessings and great things in store for you.

Message from the Author

Allow God to shine light on the things in your life that need to be dealt with. Don't live in emotional sadness or depression over your circumstances. God is there; climb Mt. God! Walk in the belief that God is 100 percent in control. Give up and raise the white flag from living for yourself, and wholly live for Him.

I leave you with this word from the Lord:

> *Do not let your emotions take over your lives. Don't say "My life is a mess" or "It's topsy-turvy." Let Me do the mess up; let Me turn your current situation upside down as I knock down the walls. Lies from the enemy will be torn down as you let go of them and lay them at My feet with confident faith. I am the healer, restorer, strength, and anything you need Me to be for each situation in which you find yourself. I am the "I am." Shadows will be lit up because nothing is hidden from My sight. I am in control when you give it to Me. You have a choice to make, and today is the day.*

Bibliography

Battista, Mike. "Deos It Mttaer Waht Oredr LTTEERS in a Wrod Are?" *CBS* blog. Online Cognitive Assessment Platform, Cambridge Brain Sciences. https://www.cambridgebrainsciences.com/more/articles/deos-it-mttaer-waht-oredr-the-ltteers-in-a-wrod-are.

"MRC Cognition and Brain Sciences Unit Using Cognitive Theory and Innovations in Neuroscience to Understand and Improve Mental Wellbeing across the Lifespan." MRC Cognition and Brain Sciences Unit, University of Cambridge. Accessed September 23, 2003. http://www.mrc-cbu.cam.ac.uk/people/matt-davis/cmabridge/.

About the Author

Jaimee Wolfard grew up in Missouri, where she was brought up attending church when the doors were open and learned to trust God no matter the circumstances. She loves serving others and praising God through song. She has many testimonies in her life where God made ways when there seemed to be no way. She earned a bachelor's degree from College of the Ozarks and a master's degree from Missouri State. She has a teaching certification in language arts as well as behavioral special education cross category.

Currently, Jaimee is walking out her calling one step at a time as God gives her directions and new revelations. She does her best to be an example of God's light and love to young students as she teaches ELA in middle school. Jaimee worships alongside her husband, Atlee, as he leads worship at Landmark Church in Strafford, Missouri. She resides in Marshfield, Missouri, with her husband, two of their three kids (two are in college, but her oldest just recently married), two individuals with specialized needs (host home individuals), her father and stepmother, as well as four dogs.

Her heart's desire is that everyone can find their passion and calling in Christ, no matter what they are going through or have been through, by strengthening their relationship with Him. Everyone has life issues but will be victorious when their lives align with His.